This book was given to

_____

By _____

Message

_____

_____

_____

Published by CHRISTIAN ART PUBLISHERS

©2003
CHRISTIAN ART PUBLISHERS
PO Box 1599, Vereeniging, 1930
South Africa

First edition 2003

Written by Lyndi Strydom
Illustrated by Rick Incrocci
Cover designed by Christian Art Publishers

Scripture taken from the *Holy Bible*, New International Version.
Copyright 1973, 1978, 1984 by International Bible Society.
Used by permission of Zondervan Publishing House. All rights reserved.

Set in 12 on 24pt Comic Sans by Christian Art Publishers

Printed in Singapore

ISBN 1-86920-232-5

03   04   05   06   07   08   09   10   11   12 – 10 9 8 7 6 5 4 3 2 1

God's Creation of Earth

CHRISTIAN ART
PUBLISHERS

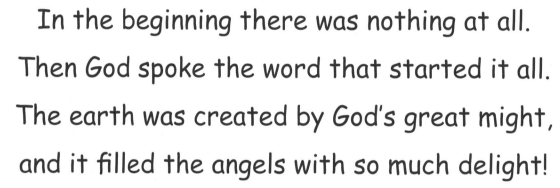

> In the beginning God created
> the heavens and the earth.
>
> GENESIS 1:1

In the beginning there was nothing at all.

Then God spoke the word that started it all.

The earth was created by God's great might,

and it filled the angels with so much delight!

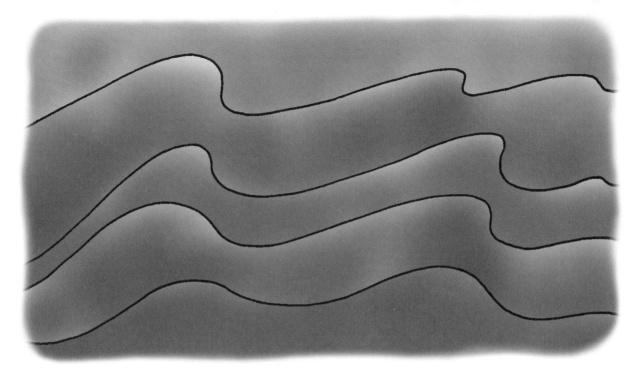

Dear God,
You started with nothing and
made everything there is. You are
amazing! Thank You for making
the earth and everything in it!
Amen.

And God said, "Let there be light,"
and there was light.

GENESIS 1:3

God started by saying, "Let there be light."

When it appeared God smiled with delight.

But God wasn't finished, He had more to say;

He called the dark "night"

and the light He called "day."

Dear God,
I play with my friends in the daytime. I have a good rest in the nighttime. Thank You for making day and night. Amen.

And God said, "Let there be an expanse between the waters to separate water from water" ... God called the expanse "sky."

GENESIS 1:6, 8

On day two God made the heavens so high;

He split water from air that fills up the sky.

Waters covered the earth, that was the sea,

and the water in clouds pours rain over me.

Dear God,
Thank You for all the different
ways You made water for us: rain
and rivers, lakes and waterfalls,
little streams and the huge sea.
Amen.

And God said, "Let the water under
the sky be gathered to one place,
and let the dry ground appear."

GENESIS 1:9

On day three water flowed free

till God called it together

and dry land you could see.

God told the seas how far they could come

and was pleased when He saw

all He had done.

Dear God,
It is fun to play in the water. It is fun to play in the sand. Thank You for holding the whole world in Your hand. Amen.

Then God said, "Let the land produce vegetation: seed-bearing plants and trees on the land that bear fruit with seeds in it."

GENESIS 1:11

On this day God looked at the land so good

and saw it was ready to grow all kinds of food.

He started creating flowers so pretty

and trees so tall

and all kinds of seeds and plants for us all.

Dear God,
It feels so good to roll on the grass and to smell flowers and to climb trees. Thank You for all the bright colors that make the world so pretty. Amen.

> Give thanks to the LORD, for he is good ...
> He gives food to every creature.
>
> PSALM 136:25

And that was the day God gave food to us all,

with apples and pear trees that grow so tall.

Every single fruit holds tiny seeds

to grow all the food we ever could need.

14

 Dear God,
Thank You for juicy apples and oranges. Thank You for providing food for us all. You are so great! Amen.

And God said, "Let there be lights in the expanse of the sky to separate the day from the night, and let them serve as signs to mark seasons and days and years."

GENESIS 1:14

On the fourth day God made the big lights

that make the difference

between days and nights.

The special lights shine from the skies on us all

and change the seasons

from spring and summer to fall.

Dear God,
At nighttime I watch the stars twinkling in the sky. I love to see how the moon changes shape, from small to big and small again. Thank You for all the wonders in the sky. Amen.

> The heavens declare the glory of God;
> the skies proclaim the work of his hands.
>
> PSALM 19:1

The daytime sky shines bright with the sun

and twinkling stars make the night sky fun.

The moon lights up the sky at night

which is always a very pretty sight.

Dear God,
The sun keeps us warm and helps plants grow big. The moon and stars keep the dark night from being scary. Thank You for making all of them! Amen.

And God said, "Let the water teem with living creatures, and let birds fly above the earth across the expanse of the sky."

GENESIS 1:20

Creatures that move, God made on day five,

He filled the waters with things all alive.

Fish swim around in the wide, wide seas

and beautiful birds chirp in the trees.

Dear God,
When I go to the sea or play near a river, I see so many funny creatures; crabs and shellfish and tiny silvery fish. Thank You for creating them all. Amen.

21

So God created the great creatures
of the sea ... and every winged bird.

GENESIS 1:21

Then God looked at the sky and saw it was bare

so He thought to fill it with birds so fair.

God looked at all the fish and birds that sing,

and He was very pleased with everything.

22

Dear God,
You had good ideas when You made different things like sea horses and whales, and hummingbirds and eagles. Thank You for everything that swims and flies. Amen.

> And God said, "Let the land produce living creatures according to their kinds."
>
> GENESIS 1:24

On day six God knew He was not yet done.

The land needed animals that could there run.

All kinds of creatures, some big and some small,

were made on that day by the God of us all.

Dear God,
It must have been fun to make kittens and puppies and elephants and giraffes. I'm glad You thought of so many animals. Amen.

> Praise the LORD from the earth you great
> sea creatures ... wild animals and all cattle,
> small creatures and flying birds.
>
> PSALM 148:7, 10

And from that day God loved to see

all the creatures of the earth and the sea.

But one thing more God wanted so much

a man in His image, made with His touch.

Dear God,
You were pleased with the things
You made. Help me to take care
of Your world and everything in it.
Amen.

So God created man in his own image, in
the image of God he created him;
male and female he created them.

GENESIS 1:27

God made the first man out of the dust

and then breathed life into him

so that in God he would trust.

But He saw that man was alone,

with no one to share his life.

Then God made him a woman

so that she could be his wife.

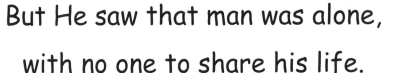

Dear God,
You saved Your best creation for last. Thank You for making people. Thank You for making me! Amen.

> The earth is the LORD's and everything
> in it, the world, and all who live in it.
>
> PSALM 24:1

God told the animals to eat from the trees

grow big and strong and roam around free.

He asked man to look after the earth so good.

"Take care of My world," and man understood.

Dear God,
Thank You for my dad and my mom, my brothers and sisters, and all my friends. Thank You that You made each one of us special. Amen.

And God blessed the seventh day and made it holy, because on it he rested from all the work of creating that he had done.

GENESIS 2:3

The seventh day God used to rest.

He set it apart and called it blessed.

After the work that took so many days

His creation worshiped Him with praise.

Dear God,
All You had to do was say the words and everything was made. You did a lot of work in six days. You deserved a good rest. Thank You for making everything. Amen.

Dear God,
With all Your creations
and the beauty we see,
I want to say thank You
because You made it for me.
The birds, fish and creatures
that so freely run,
and the flowers and plants
that grow in the sun.
The fruits of the trees
that taste so right,
the stars and the moon
that shine so bright.
Dear Heavenly Father,
I want to praise You,
for all Your love
and kind things You do. Amen.